Loving God and Others: The Heart of True Faith

Kay Arthur, David & BJ Lawson

PRECEPT MINISTRIES INTERNATIONAL

WATERBROOK

LOVING GOD AND OTHERS: THE HEART OF TRUE FAITH

All Scripture quotations, unless otherwise indicated, are taken from the *New American Standard Bible®* (NASB), © Copyright The Lockman Foundation 1960, 1962, 1963, 1968, 1971, 1972, 1973, 1975, 1977, 1995. Used by permission. (www.Lockman.org)

Trade Paperback ISBN 978-0-307-45868-1
eBook ISBN 978-0-307-45869-8

Copyright © 2009 by Precept Ministries International

Published in the United States by WaterBrook, an imprint of the Crown Publishing Group, a division of Penguin Random House LLC, New York.

WATERBROOK® and its deer colophon are registered trademarks of Penguin Random House LLC.

Printed in the United States of America
2019

20 19 18 17 16 15 14

CONTENTS

HOW TO USE THIS STUDY

This small-group study is for people who are interested in learning for themselves more about what the Bible says on various subjects, but who have only limited time to meet together. It's ideal, for example, for a lunch group at work, an early morning men's group, a young mothers' group meeting in a home, a Sunday-school class, or even family devotions. (It's also ideal for small groups that typically have longer meeting times—such as evening groups or Saturday morning groups—but want to devote only a portion of their time together to actual study, while reserving the rest for prayer, fellowship, or other activities.)

This book is designed so that all the group's participants will complete each lesson's study activities *at the same time*. Discussing your insights drawn from what God says about the subject reveals exciting, life-impacting truths.

Although it's a group study, you'll need a facilitator to lead the study and keep the discussion moving. (This person's function is *not* that of a lecturer or teacher. However, when this book is used in a Sunday-school class or similar setting, the teacher should feel free to lead more directly and to bring in other insights in addition to those provided in each week's lesson.)

If *you* are your group's facilitator, the leader, here are some helpful points for making your job easier:

- Go through the lesson and mark the text before you lead the group. This will give you increased familiarity with the material and will enable you to facilitate the group with greater ease. It may be easier for you to lead the group through the instructions for marking if you, as a leader, choose a specific color for each symbol you mark.

- As you lead the group, start at the beginning of the text and simply read it aloud in the order it appears in the lesson, including the "insight boxes," which appear throughout. Work through the lesson together, observing and discussing what you learn. As you read the Scripture verses, have the group say aloud the word they are marking in the text.

- The discussion questions are there simply to help you cover the material. As the class moves into the discussion, many times you will find that they will cover the questions on their own. Remember, the discussion questions are there to guide the group through the topic, not to squelch discussion.

- Remember how important it is for people to verbalize their answers and discoveries. This greatly strengthens their personal understanding of each week's lesson. Try to ensure that everyone has plenty of opportunity to contribute to each week's discussions.

- Keep the discussion moving. This may mean spending more time on some parts of the study than on others. If necessary, you should feel free to spread out a lesson over more than one session. However, remember that you don't want to slow the pace too much. It's much better to leave everyone "wanting more" than to have people dropping out because of declining interest.

- If the validity or accuracy of some of the answers seems questionable, you can gently and cheerfully remind the group to stay focused on the truth of the Scriptures. Your object is to learn what the Bible says, not to engage in human philosophy. Simply stick with the Scriptures and give God the opportunity to speak. His Word *is* truth (John 17:17)!

LOVING GOD
AND OTHERS:
THE HEART
OF TRUE FAITH

Have you ever asked yourself, *What does God really want from me?*

Those who truly want to please God can easily get confused. One Bible teacher details a long list of all of the commands you should be keeping. The next teacher says you are not under law at all; all that matters is grace. Does that mean you don't have to keep any commands? Who is right?

What does it take to live a God-pleasing life?

Centuries ago, the experts in Jewish law took the Ten Commandments and multiplied them into 613 laws. Talk about confusing. Jesus, however, took the

Ten Commandments and divided them into two: love God and love people.

In the next six lessons we'll look at these two great commands that define the very heart of Christian faith—and learn how following them can transform not only your life but the lives of those around you.

When an expert in the law asked which was the greatest commandment, Jesus answered by referring to the Shema, a basic confession of faith in Judaism that calls the people to love God with all of their heart, soul, mind, and strength. This answer is what the lawyer expected; however, what Jesus said next surprised His listeners and changed the course of history. Not only were God's people to love Him with all their heart, soul, mind, and strength, but they also were to love others as themselves.

OBSERVE

The religious leaders of the day had one goal: to get rid of Jesus. To that end, they had been challenging Jesus' authority. The scene we're about to look at opens just after the Sadducees tried unsuccessfully to trap Him into saying something that would get Him in trouble with the people and the Roman rulers. Now the Pharisees were trying to do the same. They sent a lawyer to Jesus with a question hotly debated among the religious leaders of the time.

Leader: *Read Matthew 22:34–40 aloud. Have the group say aloud and…*

MATTHEW 22:34–40

34 But when the Pharisees heard that Jesus had silenced the Sadducees, they gathered themselves together.

35 One of them, a lawyer, asked Him a question, testing Him,

36 "Teacher, which is the great commandment in the Law?"

37 And He said to him, " 'You shall love the LORD your God with all your heart, and with all your soul, and with all your mind.'

38 "This is the great and foremost commandment.

39 "The second is like it, 'You shall love your neighbor as yourself.'

40 "On these two commandments depend the whole Law and the Prophets."

• *mark every reference to **Jesus**, including synonyms and pronouns, with a cross:*

✝

• *draw a heart over each occurrence of the word **love**:* ♡

As you read the text, it's helpful to have the group say the key words aloud as they mark them. This way everyone will be sure they are marking every occurrence of the word, including any synonymous words or phrases. Do this throughout the study.

DISCUSS
• What did the Pharisee ask Jesus?

• What was Jesus' response?

• What did Jesus identify as the second most important commandment?

• What do we learn about these two commandments in verse 40?

INSIGHT

The phrase *the Law and the Prophets* was the standard way of referring to the Hebrew Scriptures (our Old Testament). When Jesus said, "On these two commandments depend the whole Law and the Prophets," He meant that all other commands are summed up or contained in these two.

OBSERVE

In boiling the Law down to two commands, was Jesus doing away with the rest of the Law and the Prophets?

Leader: Read Matthew 5:17–20 out loud. Have the group say and…

MATTHEW 5:17–20

17 Do not think that I came to abolish the Law or the Prophets; I did not come to abolish but to fulfill.

18 For truly I say to you, until heaven and earth pass away, not the smallest letter or stroke shall pass from the Law until all is accomplished.

19 Whoever then annuls one of the least of these commandments, and teaches others to do the same, shall be called least in the kingdom of heaven; but whoever keeps and teaches them, he shall be called great in the kingdom of heaven.

20 For I say to you that unless your righteousness surpasses that of the scribes and Pharisees, you will not enter the kingdom of heaven.

- *mark each occurrence of the pronoun **I**, which refers to **Jesus**, with a cross.*
- *draw a box around every reference to the **Law**, including pronouns and synonyms such as **commandments:*** ☐

DISCUSS

- What did you learn from marking the references to Jesus?

- What did you learn from marking the references to the Law?

- To be sure you don't miss it, what was Jesus' intent with regard to the Law?

OBSERVE

Paul, writing later, commented on what the law meant for a Christian.

Leader: Read Romans 13:8–10 aloud. Have the group…
- *draw a heart over each occurrence of the word **love**.*
- *underline each **commandment.***

DISCUSS

• Look where you marked *love* and discuss what you learned.

• What do you know about the one who loves his neighbor? How does verse 10 relate to verse 9? Explain your answer.

ROMANS 13:8–10

8 Owe nothing to anyone except to love one another; for he who loves his neighbor has fulfilled the law.

9 For this, "You shall not commit adultery, you shall not murder, you shall not steal, you shall not covet," and if there is any other commandment, it is summed up in this saying, "You shall love your neighbor as yourself."

10 Love does no wrong to a neighbor; therefore love is the fulfillment of the law.

• A line from a popular song asks, "What's love got to do with it?" So what *does* love have to do with obeying the commandments?

• So that you don't miss it, is God's highest goal for a believer simply to keep the "rules"? Explain your answer.

MARK 12:32–34

32 The scribe said to Him, "Right, Teacher; You have truly stated that He is One, and there is no one else besides Him;

33 and to love Him with all the heart and with all the understanding and with all the strength, and to

OBSERVE

The gospel of Mark expands on the same story we saw in Matthew 22. The lawyer, or scribe, is still speaking to Jesus.

Leader: Read Mark 12:32–34 aloud. Have the group do the following:
- *mark every reference to **Jesus**, including synonyms and pronouns, with a cross:* ✝
- *draw a heart over each occurrence of the word **love**:* ♡
- *underline **the two commandments** in this passage.*

DISCUSS

• What new information did you gain from reading Mark's account of this encounter?

• What insight does the end of verse 33 give us concerning the scribe? What was he beginning to understand about what matters most to God? Explain your answer.

• Discuss how this conversation between Jesus and the scribe applies to your daily life. Is there anything you need to do differently to make sure your priorities align with God's?

love one's neighbor as himself, is much more than all burnt offerings and sacrifices."

34 When Jesus saw that he had answered intelligently, He said to him, "You are not far from the kingdom of God." After that, no one would venture to ask Him any more questions.

DEUTERONOMY 6:5

You shall love the LORD your God with all your heart and with all your soul and with all your might.

LEVITICUS 19:18

You shall not take vengeance, nor bear any grudge against the sons of your people, but you shall love your neighbor as yourself; I am the LORD.

OBSERVE

Where would one get the idea to sum up all of the laws with only two commands?

Leader: Read Deuteronomy 6:5 and Leviticus 19:18.

- *Have the group say aloud and mark with a heart each occurrence of the word* **love.**

INSIGHT

One way to better understand what the text is saying is by asking the "Five Ws and an H" questions—*who, what, when, where, why,* and *how*—about the passage. By asking these questions, you slow down and actually see what the writer is saying.

DISCUSS

- What did you learn from marking *love* in Deuteronomy 6:5?

- **Who** are you to love?

• **How** are you to love Him?

• **What** does that mean? Explain your answer.

• What did you learn about love in Leviticus 19:18?

• **Who** are you to love?

• **How** are you to love them?

• **Why** are you to do this?

OBSERVE

Now let's look at the Law, the Ten Commandments.

Leader: *Read Exodus 20:3–17 aloud. Have the group...*

EXODUS 20:3–17

3 You shall have no other gods before Me.

4 You shall not make for yourself an idol, or

any likeness of what is in heaven above or on the earth beneath or in the water under the earth.

5 You shall not worship them or serve them; for I, the LORD your God, am a jealous God, visiting the iniquity of the fathers on the children, on the third and the fourth generations of those who hate Me,

6 but showing lovingkindness to thousands, to those who love Me and keep My commandments.

7 You shall not③ take the name of the LORD your God in vain, for the LORD will not leave him unpunished who takes His name in vain.

• *mark every reference to **God**, including synonyms and pronouns, with a triangle:* △
• *number each of **the Ten Commandments** in the text. The first three are already marked for you.*

DISCUSS

• Make a list of all of the commandments connected directly to our relationship with God.

• Make a list of all of the other commandments.

• What do you notice about these two lists? How could you sum up the central theme of each? How does this relate to our study?

As we bring this week's lesson to a close, review what you learned and then answer the following questions:

• What did Jesus say is the most important commandment?

• What is the second most important?

8 Remember the sabbath day, to keep it holy.

9 Six days you shall labor and do all your work,

10 but the seventh day is a sabbath of the LORD your God; in it you shall not do any work, you or your son or your daughter, your male or your female servant or your cattle or your sojourner who stays with you.

11 For in six days the LORD made the heavens and the earth, the sea and all that is in them, and rested on the seventh day; therefore the LORD blessed the sabbath day and made it holy.

12 Honor your father and your mother, that your days may be prolonged in the land which the LORD your God gives you.

13 You shall not murder.

14 You shall not commit adultery.

15 You shall not steal.

16 You shall not bear false witness against your neighbor.

17 You shall not covet your neighbor's house; you shall not covet your neighbor's wife or his male servant or his female servant or his ox or his donkey or anything that belongs to your neighbor.

• What ties the two together?

• What is the relationship between the Law and these two commandments? Explain your answer.

WRAP IT UP

This week we looked at Jesus' answer to a question that's just as hotly debated today as it was in the time of the Pharisees: what is God's most important requirement of His people? Jesus clearly said that loving God is our first obligation. But He also identified a second commandment as being foundational: Leviticus 19:18. These two commandments are the greatest of all, and the rest flow out of them.

Love is the glue that holds together not only the Law and the Prophets, but the Gospel as well. Without love, Christianity would be like every other religion with a set of rules and regulations leading to legalism and bondage rather than freedom and grace. That is what Jesus meant when He said "unless your righteousness surpasses that of the scribes and Pharisees, you will not enter the kingdom of heaven" (Matthew 5:20). The Pharisees saw the Law as a checklist to prove their righteousness. Jesus, however, identified the Law's purpose as a guide to remind us to love God and to love people. He was apparently the first to fuse these two commandments together and use them to summarize the law.

A deep sense of gratitude for what God has done for us should motivate us to love Him and others. Did you notice the word *and*? You don't get to choose your preference; both loving God and loving people are at the heart of our faith. The result of loving God is that you will love people. And loving people is the way to show the world that you love God. We must be careful not to emphasize either our devotion to God or our social concerns at the expense of the other.

In the weeks to come we will learn how to live out both of these commandments so that we can make an impact on our families, churches, communities, and ultimately our culture. Meanwhile, take a look at your life this week and ask God to show you how well you are living out of love. If He shows you changes that need to be made, write them down and begin to work on them.

What does it mean to love God? Is regular church attendance or consistent tithing an indicator of one's love for God? What does He really want from us? This week we will find the answer to these questions.

OBSERVE

As we saw in last week's lesson, the question of which is the greatest commandment was debated among the religious leaders of Jesus' day. Many different commandments were being championed as the most important.

As we start this lesson, let's briefly review some of what we learned last week from Jesus' conversation with the lawyer.

Leader: Read Matthew 22:37–38 aloud. Have the group say and…
* mark **God** with a triangle: △
* draw a heart over the word **love:** ♡

DISCUSS

• What did you learn from marking *love*?

• Who are we to love?

MATTHEW 22:37–38

37 And He said to him, " 'You shall love the LORD your God with all your heart, and with all your soul, and with all your mind.'

38 "This is the great and foremost commandment."

• How are we to love? What aspects of our lives are to be influenced by this love?

• What did Jesus say about this commandment?

EXODUS 20:2–11

² I am the LORD your God, who brought you out of the land of Egypt, out of the house of slavery.

³ You shall have no other gods ① before Me.

⁴ You shall not make ② for yourself an idol, or any likeness of what is in heaven above or on the earth beneath or in

OBSERVE

Jesus said the greatest commandment was to love God. That idea is reflected in the Law, which we would commonly call the Ten Commandments.

Leader: Read Exodus 20:2–11 aloud. Have the group say aloud and...
- *number each of* **the Ten Commandments** *in the text. The first two have been marked for you.*
- *draw a triangle over every reference to* **God,** *including synonyms and pronouns.*
- *mark the word* **love** *with a heart.*

INSIGHT

The Ten Commandments are the core of all Israel's religious and civil laws. They lay a moral foundation for a holy community. As we observed last week, the first four focus on Israel's relationship with God. The other six deal with relationships between people.

DISCUSS

• Who is speaking in these verses?

• Therefore, who is the author of the Law? Why does that matter?

• What two things did you learn about God in verse 2?

the water under the earth.

5 You shall not worship them or serve them; for I, the LORD your God, am a jealous God, visiting the iniquity of the fathers on the children, on the third and the fourth generations of those who hate Me,

6 but showing lovingkindness to thousands, to those who love Me and keep My commandments.

7 You shall ③ not take the name of the LORD your God in vain, for the LORD will not leave him unpunished who takes His name in vain.

8 Remember the sabbath day, to keep it holy.

9 Six days you shall labor and do all your work,

10 but the seventh day is a sabbath of the LORD your God; in it you shall not do any work, you or your son or your daughter, your male or your female servant or your cattle or your sojourner who stays with you.

11 For in six days the LORD made the heavens and the earth, the sea and all that is in them, and rested on the seventh day; therefore the LORD blessed the sabbath day and made it holy.

• According to verse 2, what is God's unique relationship to this people?

• According to the first commandment, what or who is to be the object of our worship?

• Discuss why the first commandment is foundational in relationship to the rest of the commandments.

• What is the second commandment?

• What did you learn about God in verses 5 and 6?

• What difference should this knowledge make in our behavior?

• What is the third commandment?

INSIGHT

The Hebrew word translated *vain* literally means "empty or without content; to be of no value, worthless." Therefore to take the Lord's name in vain would be to treat His name as worthless.

• This commandment applies not only to a believer's speech but also to his lifestyle. Discuss what obedience to this would look like in the life of a believer.

• When God's name is used in a disrespect-
ful way, do you think He notices?

• How do you feel when you hear God's
name used carelessly, without respect?

• What is the fourth commandment?

• How is the Sabbath to be observed?

• Who is to observe it, according to verse
10?

• Why is the Sabbath important, according
to verse 11?

• Taking everything into consideration,
what does it look like for you to love
God? What practical impact will that love
have on your daily life?

OBSERVE

In Matthew 22:37–38, when Jesus answered the lawyer's question, He quoted from the Shema, the basic confession of faith in Judaism. Let's look at the passage in Deuteronomy to which He referred.

Leader: Read Deuteronomy 6:4–9 aloud. Have the group say and...
- *draw a triangle over every reference to **God**, including synonyms and pronouns.*
- *mark the word **love** with a heart.*
- *draw a box around the phrase **these words** and the pronouns **them** and **they**, which refer to the words.*

DISCUSS

• What did you learn in verse 4 about God?

• What did God require of the Israelites, according to verse 5?

DEUTERONOMY 6:4–9

4 Hear, O Israel! The LORD is our God, the LORD is one!

5 You shall love the LORD your God with all your heart and with all your soul and with all your might.

6 These words, which I am commanding you today, shall be on your heart.

7 You shall teach them diligently to your sons and shall talk of them when you sit in your house and when you walk by the way and when you lie down and when you rise up.

8 You shall bind them as a sign on your hand and they shall be

as frontals on your forehead.

9 You shall write them on the doorposts of your house and on your gates.

• What did you learn from marking the references to words? What were God's people responsible to do with His words?

INSIGHT

The heart, biblically speaking, is the seat of the emotions. The soul is the center of man's personality. So love for God was to permeate the very essence of man.

God's words—not our emotions, intellect, or physical cravings—should be our guide for life.

• What role did these words play in a person's daily life? Was it enough to simply memorize them? Explain your answer.

• Paul wrote in Romans 15:4, "Whatever was written in earlier times was written for our instruction." What does that tell you about these verses from Deuteronomy?

• By considering God's words, meditating on them, and teaching them to others, how would our lives be impacted?

• In practical terms, what does it mean for you to love God with all your heart, all your soul, all your might?

OBSERVE

Farther along in Deuteronomy, we find Moses again calling Israel to total commitment to the Lord.

Leader: Read Deuteronomy 10:12–13 aloud. Have the group mark...
- *every reference to **the Lord,** including pronouns, with a triangle.*
- *the word **love** with a heart.*

DEUTERONOMY 10:12–13

12 Now, Israel, what does the LORD your God require from you, but to fear the LORD your God, to walk in all His ways and love Him, and to serve the LORD your God with all your

heart and with all your soul,

13 and to keep the LORD's commandments and His statutes which I am commanding you today for your good?

INSIGHT

Often in Bible study, it is helpful to look again at the words you've marked, to note what the text says about those words. This helps you understand what the text is saying.

DISCUSS

• Make a list of the five things the Lord required of Israel.

• Discuss the requirements you listed above. What does each mean? Would any of them apply to us today and, if so, how?

• From what you saw in this passage, what is the evidence that a person fears and loves God?

• What reason is given in verse 13 for being totally committed to God's ways?

OBSERVE

Let's look at a man whose love for God was put to the test. After waiting about twenty-five years, Abraham finally held in his arms the son God had promised. A few years later, he faced the most difficult test of his life, a test designed to prove his faith.

Leader: Read Genesis 22:1–8 aloud. Have the group mark…
* *each reference to **Abraham,** including pronouns, with a big **A.***
* *each mention of **Isaac,** including pronouns and synonyms, with a big **I.***

DISCUSS

• What did God instruct Abraham to do? How was this a test of his faith? (See the Insight box on page 28 if you need help.)

GENESIS 22:1–8

¹ Now it came about after these things, that God tested Abraham, and said to him, "Abraham!" And he said, "Here I am."

² He said, "Take now your son, your only son, whom you love, Isaac, and go to the land of Moriah, and offer him there as a burnt offering on one of the mountains of which I will tell you."

³ So Abraham rose early in the morning and saddled his donkey, and took two of his young men with

him and Isaac his son; and he split wood for the burnt offering, and arose and went to the place of which God had told him.

4 On the third day Abraham raised his eyes and saw the place from a distance.

5 Abraham said to his young men, "Stay here with the donkey, and I and the lad will go over there; and we will worship and return to you."

6 Abraham took the wood of the burnt offering and laid it on Isaac his son, and he took in his hand the fire and the knife. So the two of them walked on together.

• What was Abraham's response, according to verse 3?

INSIGHT

God had made a covenant with Abraham twenty-five years prior to the birth of Isaac, promising him descendants, land, and a great nation, and declaring that all the families on the earth would be blessed through him. Isaac was the promised son of the covenant. It was through Isaac that all these things would come to pass.

• What did Abraham's actions reveal about his relationship with God?

OBSERVE

Let's continue on in the story.

Leader: *Read Genesis 22:9–14 aloud. Have the group mark...*

- *each reference to **Abraham**, including pronouns, with an* **A.**
- *each mention of **Isaac**, including pronouns and synonyms, with an* **I.**

GENESIS 22:9–14

7 Isaac spoke to Abraham his father and said, "My father!" And he said, "Here I am, my son." And he said, "Behold, the fire and the wood, but where is the lamb for the burnt offering?"

8 Abraham said, "God will provide for Himself the lamb for the burnt offering, my son." So the two of them walked on together.

9 Then they came to the place of which God had told him; and Abraham built the altar there and arranged the wood, and bound his son Isaac and laid him on the altar, on top of the wood.

10 Abraham stretched out his hand and took the knife to slay his son.

11 But the angel of the LORD called to him from heaven and said, "Abraham, Abraham!" And he said, "Here I am."

12 He said, "Do not stretch out your hand against the lad, and do nothing to him; for now I know that you fear God, since you have not withheld your son, your only son, from Me."

13 Then Abraham raised his eyes and looked, and behold, behind him a ram caught in the thicket by his horns; and Abraham went and

DISCUSS

• How did Abraham measure up in the test he was given? What did his words and actions prove?

• Keeping in mind what you saw in this passage and the Insight box earlier in this lesson, discuss how Abraham demonstrated that he loved the Lord with all his heart and with all his soul and all his strength.

• What about you? What evidence can others see in your life that declares the same about you?

took the ram and offered him up for a burnt offering in the place of his son.

14 Abraham called the name of that place The LORD Will Provide, as it is said to this day, "In the mount of the LORD it will be provided."

WRAP IT UP

The decision to be a Christ-follower begins with a profound sense of gratitude for what God has done for us in Christ. To truly love God is to totally commit your life to Him. The love for God we have seen in this lesson is not a warm, fuzzy feeling; it is a love expressed in action—in serving and obeying. This love involves an absolute surrender that dominates your emotions, directs your thoughts, and determines your actions.

Relationship with God is not achieved by attending church or by going through the rituals and motions of religion. Our love for God is best expressed through our undivided allegiance and with our whole heart. As we study the Word of God and learn who He is and what He has done for us, the natural result will be to love Him with all of our heart, all of our soul, all of our might. This kind of love will so permeate our being that our lifestyle and our worldview will be totally, radically focused on Him. And everyone around us will see it.

Love is an action word. We show our love for God by obeying His words. How else would our love for God be measured? How are you doing? In what ways is your love for God evident in your life?

We've looked at the greatest commandment and what it really means to love God. This week we'll turn our attention to the second greatest commandment and consider what it requires of us.

OBSERVE

Although He was asked only about the greatest commandment, Jesus wanted His disciples to know that loving God isn't the sole requirement of right living.

Leader: Read Matthew 22:39 and Leviticus 19:18. Have the group say aloud and...
- *draw a heart over the word **love:*** ♡
- *mark each occurrence of the word* ***neighbor** with an* **N.**

MATTHEW 22:39

The second is like it, "You shall love your neighbor as yourself."

LEVITICUS 19:18

You shall not take vengeance, nor bear any grudge against the sons of your people, but you shall love your neighbor as yourself; I am the LORD.

DISCUSS

- What is the second most important commandment?

- What additional insight does the Leviticus passage give you about this commandment?

LUKE 10:25–29

25 And a lawyer stood up and put Him to the test, saying, "Teacher, what shall I do to inherit eternal life?"

26 And He said to him, "What is written in the Law? How does it read to you?"

27 And he answered, "You shall love the LORD your God with all your heart, and with all your soul, and with all your strength, and with all your mind; and your neighbor as yourself."

28 And He said to him, "You have answered correctly; do this and you will live."

• According to Leviticus 19:18, how are we to love our neighbor? What does that look like?

OBSERVE

The logical question then is, "Who is my neighbor?" Exactly who are we supposed to love? And that is precisely the question Jesus was asked.

Leader: Read Luke 10:25–29 aloud. Have the group...

- *draw a circle around each reference to* (the lawyer,) *including pronouns.*
- *mark every reference to* **Jesus,** *including pronouns and the synonym* **Teacher,** *with a cross:* ✝
- *mark each occurrence of the word* **neighbor** *with an* **N.**

DISCUSS

• Discuss what you learned from marking the references to the lawyer and to Jesus. Remember to ask the "Five Ws and an H"— who, what, when, where, why, and how.

- The lawyer had given the correct answer to Jesus' question, but was knowing the answer enough? What point did Jesus make in verse 28?

- Having felt the sting of Jesus' comment, rather than face the real issue, the lawyer felt he must justify himself. He responded as a lawyer, using a debating tactic of defining terms. What term did he want defined?

OBSERVE

Jesus answered the lawyer's question by telling a parable. As you read His story, keep in mind that the road from Jerusalem to Jericho was notoriously dangerous.

Leader: Read Luke 10:30–37. Have the group say aloud and mark each of the following words, including their pronouns, as noted:
- *draw a box around each reference to the man.*
- *mark references to the priest with a P.*
- *mark references to the Levite with an L.*
- *mark references to the Samaritan with an S.*

LUKE 10:30–37

29 But wishing to justify himself, he said to Jesus, "And who is my neighbor?"

30 Jesus replied and said, "A man was going down from Jerusalem to Jericho, and fell among robbers, and they stripped him and beat him, and went away leaving him half dead.

31 "And by chance a priest was going down on that road, and when he saw him, he passed by on the other side.

32 "Likewise a Levite also, when he came to the place and saw him, passed by on the other side.

33 "But a Samaritan, who was on a journey, came upon him; and when he saw him, he felt compassion,

34 and came to him and bandaged up his wounds, pouring oil and wine on them; and he put him on his own beast, and brought him to an inn and took care of him.

35 "On the next day he took out two denarii and gave them to the innkeeper and

Leader: Now, to be sure the class catches the flow of thought, read this passage aloud once more without stopping to mark.

DISCUSS

• Discuss the events in verses 30–32.

INSIGHT

The priests were descendants of Aaron, who was a Levite, and they were responsible for the sacrifices and offerings in the temple.

The Levites were descendants of Levi but not necessarily of Aaron. Many of them assisted the priests.

In contrast to these respected religious leaders, Samaritans were viewed by the Jews as inferior, even repulsive, because of their mixed Jewish and Gentile ancestry. The Jews and Samaritans were enemies.

• Verse 33 starts with the word *but,* which shows a contrast. Who or what is the Samaritan contrasted with?

• What do we know about the identity of the man lying in the road? (Hint: He was coming down from Jerusalem.)

• Who helped him?

• From what you read in the Insight box, why is it significant that the priest and Levite ignored the man's need? What is noteworthy about the man who responded?

• List all that the Samaritan did for the man he found.

said, 'Take care of him; and whatever more you spend, when I return I will repay you.'

36 "Which of these three do you think proved to be a neighbor to the man who fell into the robbers' hands?"

37 And he said, "The one who showed mercy toward him." Then Jesus said to him, "Go and do the same."

• Discuss how his actions relate to what Jesus identified as the second greatest commandment in Matthew 22:39.

• After describing how three different people responded to the man in need, what did Jesus ask the lawyer?

• How did the lawyer answer?

• What did Jesus then tell him to do?

• From all you have learned from this passage discuss how Jesus' story answers the question, *Who is my neighbor?*

• What if the person in need is of a different race? Political party? Economic status?
An enemy? What is our response to be?

OBSERVE

Jesus, in His Sermon on the Mount,
explained that He came to fulfill the Law.
He then went on to explain the intent of
the Law in ways His listeners had never
before considered.

*Leader: Read Matthew 5:43–44 aloud.
Have the group...*
  • *mark each occurrence of the word love
    with a heart.*
  • *draw a box around every reference to
    enemies, including synonyms.*

43 You have heard
that it was said, "You
shall love your neigh-
bor and hate your
enemy."

44 But I say to you,
love your enemies and
pray for those who
persecute you.

DISCUSS

• Again we see the word *but* in verse 44.
Discuss the contrast that is being made
between verses 43 and 44.

• What did you learn from marking each reference to enemies?

• By loving your enemy, what would you be demonstrating? Explain your answer.

LUKE 6:27–28

27 But I say to you who hear, love your enemies, do good to those who hate you,

28 bless those who curse you, pray for those who mistreat you.

OBSERVE

In this sermon Jesus taught that true righteousness is revealed by treating others with love. The actions He described don't come naturally; they require supernatural enabling, through the power of the Holy Spirit in the believer's life.

Leader: Read Luke 6:27–28 aloud. Have the group say and...
- *mark each occurrence of the word **love** with a heart.*
- *draw a box around every reference to **enemies**, including synonyms.*

INSIGHT

The Greek word for *love* used in this passage is *agapao*, which describes an unconditional love. This love is a choice, an act of the will. *Agape* love keeps in mind the highest good of the one being loved.

DISCUSS

• Who are we as believers called to love in these verses?

• What specific actions will this love prompt us to take? Make a list of the instructions given.

• Look at the list you have made and discuss how each instruction could be worked out practically in the life of a believer.

• Do you have any enemies—people who seem determined to make your life difficult? How do you normally deal with them?

• How will you deal with them in the future, in light of what you've learned so far this week?

| ACTS 7:54–60 | OBSERVE |

54 Now when they heard this, they were cut to the quick, and they began gnashing their teeth at him.

55 But being full of the Holy Spirit, he [Stephen] gazed intently into heaven and saw the glory of God, and Jesus standing at the right hand of God;

OBSERVE

Stephen, a righteous man in the early church, preached a powerful sermon to the Jewish leaders, showing that all through history the Jewish people had rebelled against God. The sermon cost him his life.

Leader: Read Acts 7:54–60 aloud. Have the group...
- *circle every synonym, such as **the witnesses**, and every pronoun, such as **they**, that refers to **the religious leaders**.*
- *mark every reference to **Stephen**, including pronouns, with an **S**.*

DISCUSS

• How did the religious leaders respond to Stephen's message?

• Look again at verse 60. Why are Stephen's words here extraordinary? What was happening as he spoke them?

• Immediately after he called out to the Lord, what happened?

INSIGHT

Fell asleep is a common New Testament euphemism for death.

---

56 and he said, "Behold, I see the heavens opened up and the Son of Man standing at the right hand of God."

57 But they cried out with a loud voice, and covered their ears and rushed at him with one impulse.

58 When they had driven him out of the city, they began stoning him; and the witnesses laid aside their robes at the feet of a young man named Saul.

59 They went on stoning Stephen as he called on the Lord and said, "Lord Jesus, receive my spirit!"

60 Then falling on his knees, he cried out with a loud voice, "Lord, do not hold this sin against them!" Having said this, he fell asleep.

• In what ways did Stephen's actions throughout this passage reveal both love for God and love for his neighbor?

JOHN 15:17

This I command you, that you love one another.

OBSERVE

Let's look at a verse in which Jesus was speaking to the disciples about their relationship with one another.

Leader: Read John 15:17 aloud.
  • *Have the group say aloud and mark the word* **love** *with a heart.*

DISCUSS

• Whom did Jesus tell His disciples to love?

WRAP IT UP

Did you notice the order of the commandments? First love God and then love people. We are called to be a light shining in the darkness, a people offering hope to a hopeless world. What in your life shows that you are in love with God? Going to church? Giving money? Friend, it is loving people.

Loving people is tough. It is hard work. The lawyer understood the implications of the two commands, which is why he tried to get out of obeying. He may have been thinking, *I just need to be careful what neighborhood I live in.* But Jesus' answer shows that the real question is, *Am I behaving as a neighbor?* It was not new information that the lawyer needed but a new heart. It is only when we love God that man becomes lovable.

Stephen, a man in love with God, a man filled with the Holy Spirit, a man with a new heart, prayed for the people who were killing him. Now that is love.

Love is also about meeting needs. How do we show the world the love of God? By meeting the needs of the people around us. Are you meeting needs in the lives of the people God brings into your life? Are you loving God by loving your neighbor?

Ask God to show you how to meet the needs of your family, your co-workers, even your neighbors. Then go out there and love your neighbor as yourself.

Many of us have little trouble feeling compassion for the non-Christian who has not yet encountered God's life-changing grace, but we quickly take offense at our Christian brothers and sisters and find it incredibly hard to move past our disagreements with them.

We know we should love and pray for our enemies, but what about the Christian who doesn't worship the way we do or appreciate our music or even dress like us at church?

OBSERVE

Really knowing God totally changes our lives.

Leader: Read 1 John 2:3–6 aloud. Have the group say aloud and...
- *underline each occurrence of the phrase* ***have come to know Him.***
- *draw a box around each mention of* ***commandments*** *and* ***His word.***
- *mark the word* ***love*** *with a heart:* ♡

DISCUSS

- What is the major characteristic of someone who knows God?

1 John 2:3–6

3 By this we know that we have come to know Him, if we keep His commandments.

4 The one who says, "I have come to know Him," and does not keep His commandments, is a liar, and the truth is not in him;

5 but whoever keeps His word, in him the love of God has truly been perfected. By this we know that we are in Him:

6 the one who says he abides in Him ought himself to walk in the same manner as He walked.

• Does this passage teach that we become Christians by keeping God's commandments? Explain your answer.

• As noted earlier, often in Scripture the word *but* points to a contrast between two things. What is being contrasted in verses 4 and 5, and what do you learn from this comparison?

• According to verse 6, what should be the natural result of our relationship with God?

1 JOHN 2:7–11

7 Beloved, I am not writing a new commandment to you, but an old commandment which you have had from the beginning; the old commandment is the word which you have heard.

OBSERVE

In this next passage the apostle John refers to the same commands Jesus identified in His response to the lawyer's question about the greatest commandment in Matthew 22.

Leader: *Read 1 John 2:7–11 aloud. Have the group…*
  • *draw a box around each occurrence of the word* **commandment***.*

- *mark each occurrence of the word **hates** with heart with a slash through it, like this:*
- *draw a heart over the word **loves**.*

DISCUSS

- What did you learn from marking *commandment*?

- What command is John referring to here? (Keep in mind what you learned in week 1.)

INSIGHT

John uses the word *brother* in this passage to refer to fellow believers. Once again, this love is *agape,* the kind that is unconditional, having the highest good of the object loved in mind. It is not an optional love; it comes out of duty, an act of the will.

---

8 On the other hand, I am writing a new commandment to you, which is true in Him and in you, because the darkness is passing away and the true Light is already shining.

9 The one who says he is in the Light and yet hates his brother is in the darkness until now.

10 The one who loves his brother abides in the Light and there is no cause for stumbling in him.

11 But the one who hates his brother is in the darkness and walks in the darkness, and does not know where he is going because the darkness has blinded his eyes.

• What did you learn from these verses about the person who hates his brother?

• According to verse 9, is merely saying you love your fellow Christian real love? Explain your answer.

• What did you learn from verse 10 about the one who loves his brother?

• If that is true of the one who loves his brother, then what impact would an unloving believer have on those around him?

• Why is it so important to exercise love in our interactions with fellow Christians?

OBSERVE

Jesus set a clear standard for how He expected His disciples to treat one another.

Leader: *Read John 13:34 and 15:12 aloud. Have the group say and...*
- *draw a box around each occurrence of the word* **commandment.**
- *mark the words* **love** *and* **loved** *with a heart.*

DISCUSS

• What commandment did Jesus give in these two verses?

• What is to be the standard of that love? In other words, who is our example of what true love looks like?

• What are some specific ways Jesus demonstrated love for others?

JOHN 13:34

A new commandment I give to you, that you love one another, even as I have loved you, that you also love one another.

JOHN 15:12

This is My commandment, that you love one another, just as I have loved you.

ROMANS 12:10, 16

10 Be devoted to one another in brotherly love; give preference to one another in honor....

16 Be of the same mind toward one another; do not be haughty in mind, but associate with the lowly. Do not be wise in your own estimation.

ROMANS 14:13

Therefore let us not judge one another anymore, but rather determine this—not to put an obstacle or a stumbling block in a brother's way.

ROMANS 15:7, 14

7 Therefore, accept one another, just as Christ also accepted us to the glory of God....

OBSERVE

Christian love is not a warm, fuzzy feeling you get while attending a worship service; it is something practical, with clear real-life results. Let's look together at some "one another" statements that reveal exactly how we are to put our love into practice.

Leader: Read the following verses aloud, starting with Romans 12:10, 16 and ending with 1 Peter 4:9.

- *Have the group say and underline each occurrence of the phrase one another.*

DISCUSS

- Discuss each verse and how it applies to the daily life of a believer. Keep in mind questions like:

- Who do these verses address?

- What specific actions are we, as believers, suppose to be taking?

• What specific behaviors are we to avoid?

• Why are these things important?

• Practically speaking, how can we exhibit these behaviors in relation to each of the following:

our family?

our church?

our neighbors?

14 And concerning you, my brethren, I myself also am convinced that you yourselves are full of goodness, filled with all knowledge and able also to admonish one another.

1 THESSALONIANS 5:11

Therefore encourage one another and build up one another, just as you also are doing.

GALATIANS 6:2

Bear one another's burdens, and thereby fulfill the law of Christ.

1 PETER 1:22

Since you have in obedience to the truth purified your souls for a sincere love of the brethren, fervently love one another from the heart.

1 PETER 4:9

Be hospitable to one another without complaint.

1 JOHN 3:14

We know that we have passed out of death into life, because we love the brethren. He who does not love abides in death.

JOHN 13:35

By this all men will know that you are My disciples, if you have love for one another.

our co-workers?

OBSERVE

Leader: Read 1 John 3:14 and John 13:35 aloud.

- *Have the group say aloud and mark each occurrence of the word **love** with a heart.*

DISCUSS

- What did you learn about love from these verses?

- What does a love for other believers—or lack of love—reveal about a person?

- So how important is love in the life of a believer? Explain your answer.

OBSERVE

Leader: *Read 1 Thessalonians 4:9 aloud.*

- *Have the group say aloud and mark each occurrence of the word **love** with a heart.*

DISCUSS

- How does a follower of Christ know of his or her responsibility to love other believers?

- Can any believer claim ignorance about the importance of love? Why or why not?

- In light of the commandment to love one another, what should you do about those in your life who are difficult to love?

1 THESSALONIANS 4:9

Now as to the love of the brethren, you have no need for anyone to write to you, for you yourselves are taught by God to love one another.

1 CORINTHIANS 13:3–8

³ And if I give all my possessions to feed the poor, and if I surrender my body to be burned, but do not have love, it profits me nothing.

⁴ Love is patient, love is kind and is not jealous; love does not brag and is not arrogant,

⁵ does not act unbecomingly; it does not seek its own, is not provoked, does not take into account a wrong suffered,

⁶ does not rejoice in unrighteousness, but rejoices with the truth;

⁷ bears all things, believes all things, hopes all things, endures all things.

⁸ Love never fails.

OBSERVE

As we bring this lesson to a close, let's look at one of the best descriptions of Christian love.

Leader: Read 1 Corinthians 13:3–8 aloud.
  • *Have the group say aloud and mark every reference to* **love,** *including pronouns, with a heart.*

DISCUSS

• What did you learn about the relationship between love and good works in verse 3? Explain your answer.

• Look at every place you marked *love.* Discuss each description and the practical ways it can be applied in a believer's life.

WRAP IT UP

Christian love is not a warm, fuzzy feeling that believers try to "work up" so they can get along with one another. It is a matter of the *will* rather than an *emotion*. It is a matter of determining—of making up your mind—that you will allow God's love to reach others through you, and then acting toward them in loving ways. You are not to act "as if" you love them; you act *because* you love them. This is not hypocrisy; it is obedience to God.

Jesus does not ask us to do something that He has not already done Himself. He demonstrated love by the very life that He lived. He hated all sin and disobedience, but He never hated the people who committed such sins. Even His righteous announcements of judgment always included an undercurrent of love.

Think of Jesus' love for the twelve disciples. They must have broken His heart as they argued over who was the greatest or tried to keep people from seeing Him. Each was different from the others, yet Jesus loved each one in a personal, understanding way. He was patient with Peter's impulsiveness and even with Thomas's unbelief. When Jesus commanded His disciples to love one another, He was only telling them to do as He had done. In effect, Jesus said to them—and to us— "I lived by this great commandment, and I can enable you to follow My example."

It is easy to practice a Christianity of words—singing the right songs, using the right vocabulary, praying the right prayers—yet through it all deceiving ourselves into thinking we are pleasing God.

But we challenge you to ask yourself, *How do I respond when a brother or sister in Christ doesn't meet the standard I expect?* This is the true test for the believer!

You say you are a Christian? Prove it. Let the world see you loving the people around you in real and practical ways.

OBSERVE

Leader: Read 1 John 3:1–3 aloud. Have the group say and...

- *draw a heart over each occurrence of the word **love:*** ♡
- *circle every word or phrase that refers to **children of God**, including pronouns and synonyms such as **us, we,** and **beloved.***

DISCUSS

- What did you learn about believers from this passage? (Hint: Look at each place you circled a word or phrase.)

INSIGHT

God's love for us is unique. While we were His enemies God loved us and sent His son to die for us! Our salvation began with the love of God.

1 JOHN 3:1–3

1 See how great a love the Father has bestowed on us, that we would be called children of God; and such we are. For this reason the world does not know us, because it did not know Him.

2 Beloved, now we are children of God, and it has not appeared as yet what we will be. We know that when He appears, we will be like Him, because we will see Him just as He is.

3 And everyone who has this hope fixed on Him purifies himself, just as He is pure.

• According to verse 3, what will those who have fixed their hope on Christ do?

1 JOHN 3:4–10

4 Everyone who practices sin also practices lawlessness; and sin is lawlessness.

5 You know that He appeared in order to take away sins; and in Him there is no sin.

6 No one who abides in Him sins; no one who sins has seen Him or knows Him.

7 Little children, make sure no one deceives you; the one who practices righteousness is righteous, just as He is righteous;

8 the one who practices sin is of the devil;

OBSERVE

Let's look next at a passage in which John emphasized some basics of Christianity to counteract false teachers who were attempting to pervert the fundamentals of the faith.

Leader: Read 1 John 3:4–10 aloud. Have the group do the following:
- *draw a big* **X** *over every reference to* ***sin(s).***
- *mark the words* ***righteous*** *and* ***righteousness*** *with an* **R.**
- *draw a heart over each occurrence of the word* ***love.***

DISCUSS

• What did you learn from marking *sin(s)* in these verses?

• From all you have seen in these verses, what is the mark of a true believer? What is the distinguishing characteristic of his or her lifestyle?

INSIGHT

The word *practice* conveys the idea of habitual action, not single instances.

• What did you learn about the one who doesn't love his brother?

• What two kinds of children exist in the world?

• What distinguishes these two "families" from each other?

• Are their characteristics difficult to detect?

for the devil has sinned from the beginning. The Son of God appeared for this purpose, to destroy the works of the devil.

⁹ No one who is born of God practices sin, because His seed abides in him; and he cannot sin, because he is born of God.

¹⁰ By this the children of God and the children of the devil are obvious: anyone who does not practice righteousness is not of God, nor the one who does not love his brother.

1 John 3:11-18

11 For this is the message which you have heard from the beginning, that we should love one another;

12 not as Cain, who was of the evil one and slew his brother. And for what reason did he slay him? Because his deeds were evil, and his brother's were righteous.

13 Do not be surprised, brethren, if the world hates you.

14 We know that we have passed out of death into life, because we love the brethren. He who does not love abides in death.

15 Everyone who hates his brother is a murderer; and you

OBSERVE

Leader: *Read 1 John 3:11–18 aloud. Have the group...*

- *draw a heart over each occurrence of the word* ***love***.
- *mark* ***does not love*** *and* ***hates*** *with heart with a slash through it, like this:*

DISCUSS

- What was the message "heard from the beginning"?

- What example did John use to help his readers fully understand that message? What specific relevance does that story have for us today?

- We continue to see the contrast between the children of God and the children of the devil. Discuss what you've learned about the character of each group and how they differ from each other.

• What two words did John use to sum up the character of these groups?

• Let's get to the practical application. According to verses 16 and 17, how is this love demonstrated? Discuss ways you can take these truths and apply them to your daily life.

• What is being contrasted in verse 18?

• Discuss how this distinction should affect our daily choices.

OBSERVE

The following is an example of what John described in the previous passage as loving someone "with word or with tongue."

know that no murderer has eternal life abiding in him.

16 We know love by this, that He laid down His life for us; and we ought to lay down our lives for the brethren.

17 But whoever has the world's goods, and sees his brother in need and closes his heart against him, how does the love of God abide in him?

18 Little children, let us not love with word or with tongue, but in deed and truth.

JAMES 2:15–16

15 If a brother or sister is without clothing and in need of daily food,

16 and one of you says to them, "Go in peace, be warmed and be filled," and yet you do not give them what is necessary for their body, what use is that?

Leader: Read James 2:15–16 aloud. Have the group…

- *underline each reference to **brother or sister**, including the pronouns **them** and **their.***
- *circle each occurrence of the word* **you.**

DISCUSS

- From this example what does it mean to love with word only?

- Contrast this with what it means to love in deed and truth.

INSIGHT

To love *with word or with tongue* means to love insincerely. This is the opposite of loving *in truth*, which means to genuinely love a person from the heart. In other words, simply saying "I love you" doesn't make it true. Authentic love directs one to action.

OBSERVE

People know when others are not sincere, but they are attracted by genuine love. Not only was Jesus the perfect example of this, but He also calls us to reach beyond our social comfort zone to love those whom others might view as outsiders.

Leader: *Read Matthew 9:9–13 and Luke 15:1–2 aloud. Have the group say and…*

• *mark each reference to **Jesus**, including pronouns and synonyms such as **your Teacher** and **this man**, with a cross:*

✝

• *draw a large* **P** *over each reference to* **the Pharisees**, *including pronouns.*

DISCUSS

• Who was coming to Jesus and why?

• Were these people the ones that you would expect to be hanging out with Jesus? Why do you think they were there? Explain your answers.

MATTHEW 9:9–13

⁹ As Jesus went on from there, He saw a man called Matthew, sitting in the tax collector's booth; and He said to him, "Follow Me!" And he got up and followed Him.

¹⁰ Then it happened that as Jesus was reclining at the table in the house, behold, many tax collectors and sinners came and were dining with Jesus and His disciples.

¹¹ When the Pharisees saw this, they said to His disciples, "Why is your Teacher eating with the tax collectors and sinners?"

¹² But when Jesus heard this, He said, "It

is not those who are healthy who need a physician, but those who are sick.

13 "But go and learn what this means: 'I desire compassion, and not sacrifice,' for I did not come to call the righteous, but sinners."

LUKE 15:1–2

1 Now all the tax collectors and the sinners were coming near Him to listen to Him.

2 Both the Pharisees and the scribes began to grumble, saying, "This man receives sinners and eats with them."

• Remember we saw in an earlier lesson that, although the Pharisees and the scribes were outwardly doing all the right things, they were not doing them from the heart. How did they react to Jesus' choice of companions?

• What do the comments of the Pharisees and scribes reveal about them?

• How does this relate to what we have already seen in this lesson?

• What might it cost you to exercise the kind of love that Jesus demonstrated in these passages?

• Discuss some scenarios where it might cost a believer greatly to love individuals whom others have deemed unacceptable or unworthy.

OBSERVE

Leader: *Read 1 John 3:23–24 aloud. Have the group...*

- *draw a box around the words **commandment(s)** and **commanded.***
- *draw a squiggly line under each occurrence of the word **abides,** like this:*

~~~~~~~

DISCUSS

- What does God command us to do?

- What did you learn about the one who keeps God's commandments? What does it prove?

---

1 JOHN 3:23–24

23 This is His commandment, that we believe in the name of His Son Jesus Christ, and love one another, just as He commanded us.

24 The one who keeps His commandments abides in Him, and He in him. We know by this that He abides in us, by the Spirit whom He has given us.

WRAP IT UP

John was very concerned that Christians know how to tell true believers from false ones. He presented tests throughout his letter to help determine the genuineness of one's claims to be a believer. He even went so far as to say that the children of God and the children of the devil are obvious, identified by the differences in how they behave and how they love (1 John 3:10).

Love does not define God, but God defines love. As believers, the Holy Spirit of God resides in us; therefore we should be the expression of the love of God. It is not enough to simply tell others "I love you"; we must demonstrate it by meeting their needs. It would have been a terrible thing if God had simply said that He loved the world and yet did not send His Son to die on the cross. Or if He were to say He forgave us but then refused to have anything to do with us.

Don't just say you love someone; prove it! Loving others with God's love often involves a sacrifice of time, emotions, possessions, and more. But in light of the sacrifice God made for us by sending His Son, our choice to love others demonstrates our gratefulness to Him and will be a sacrifice well worth making.

Did you know that a believer's relationship to other believers cannot be divorced from his prayer life? If husbands and wives are not obeying God's Word, for example, their prayers will be hindered (1 Peter 3:7). Love is the fulfillment of the Law (Romans 13:8–10); therefore, when you love the brethren, you are obeying God's commandments; you're living in His will where He is able to answer your requests (1 John 3:22). If it seems as if God has been ignoring your prayers, perhaps you should take inventory of your relationships and see if there is anyone whom you are not loving.

How are you loving the people around you—including the ones who make you uncomfortable?

The two great commands, to love God and to love people, sum up the whole of the Law and the Prophets. We have looked at what these commands mean and how they apply to our daily lives. But before we can live them out, there is one absolute truth—one *vital* truth—we must understand.

OBSERVE

We have talked a lot about love, but to really understand love we must start with God. Let's look at two passages that show why.

In the first passage Jesus is talking to Nicodemus, a Pharisee, a religious leader in Israel.

Leader: Read John 3:16 and 1 John 4:9–10. Have the group say aloud and...

- *mark every reference to **God**, including pronouns, with a triangle:* △
- *draw a heart over each occurrence of* ***love(d):*** ♡

DISCUSS

- Who did God love? Who is included in that?

JOHN 3:16

For God so loved the world, that He gave His only begotten Son, that whoever believes in Him shall not perish, but have eternal life.

1 JOHN 4:9–10

9 By this the love of God was manifested in us, that God has sent His only begotten Son into the world so that we might live through Him.

10 In this is love, not that we loved God,

but that He loved us and sent His Son to be the propitiation for our sins.

• How did He show His love, and why?

INSIGHT

The Greek word for *love* here is *agape*. As you have seen in earlier lessons, it is an unconditional love that has the highest good of the other person in mind. Later we will see this word used in 1 John 4 to describe God.

ROMANS 3:23

For all have sinned and fall short of the glory of God.

ROMANS 6:23

For the wages of sin is death, but the free gift of God is eternal life in Christ Jesus our Lord.

OBSERVE

Leader: *Read Romans 3:23 and 6:23.*

> • *Have the group say and draw a big* **X** *over* **sinned** *and* **sin.**

INSIGHT

The word *sin* used in these verses carries the idea of missing the standard. A standard of right was set by God, but we did not live up to the standard. We sinned.

DISCUSS

• What did you learn from marking *sin* in these two verses?

• Has there ever been a point in your life when you admitted you had done things that were wrong? Have you ever admitted that you did not live up to God's standard of righteousness?

• What is the penalty for failing to measure up to God's standard?

• What penalty have you personally earned for sinning against God?

• What is God's gift?

• If it is a gift, what can you do to earn it?

• Although you can't earn it, you must reach out to receive it. If you are not a believer, the way you do this is to ask God to forgive you and make you His child.

1 PETER 2:24

And He Himself bore our sins in His body on the cross, so that we might die to sin and live to righteousness; for by His wounds you were healed.

OBSERVE

The apostle Peter described the cost Jesus paid to show us His love.

Leader: Read 1 Peter 2:24.

*• Have the group say and circle the pronouns referring to those whom God loves: **our, we,** and **you.***

DISCUSS

• What did you learn about all of us from this passage?

• What exactly did Jesus do for us?

OBSERVE

Leader: Read Romans 5:8. Have the group...
- *mark every reference to **God**, including pronouns, with a triangle.*
- *draw a heart over the word **love**.*

DISCUSS

• How did God show that He loves us, and when did He do that?

• What was our status when God showed His love for us?

• Why did Christ have to die?

ROMANS 5:8

But God demonstrates His own love toward us, in that while we were yet sinners, Christ died for us.

ROMANS 10:9–10, 13

⁹ If you confess with your mouth Jesus as Lord, and believe in your heart that God raised Him from the dead, you will be saved;

¹⁰ for with the heart a person believes, resulting in righteousness, and with the mouth he confesses, resulting in salvation....

¹³ for "Whoever will call on the name of the LORD will be saved."

OBSERVE

Leader: *Read Romans 10:9–10, and 13. Have the group say and...*
- *mark each reference to **Jesus**, including pronouns, with a cross:* ✝
- *draw an **S** over the words **saved** and **salvation.***

INSIGHT

The words *saved* and *salvation* in the Bible mean "to be saved from the penalty of sin, or death, and to be saved from being separated from God for all eternity."

DISCUSS

• What is required for salvation, according to these verses?

• What will the results be if you believe with your heart and confess Jesus as Lord?

• If Jesus is Lord, or God, how would that reality affect your own life?

• What saves us? Religion? Church membership? Being good? Explain your answer.

OBSERVE

Leader: Read Matthew 16:24–25.

• *Have the group circle* **anyone, he, himself,** *and* **his,** *referring to those who would follow Christ.*

DISCUSS

• What are the implications of following Jesus? In other words, what does it cost someone to follow Jesus?

MATTHEW 16:24–25

24 Then Jesus said to His disciples, "If anyone wishes to come after Me, he must deny himself, and take up his cross and follow Me.

25 "For whoever wishes to save his life will lose it; but whoever loses his life for My sake will find it.

• From what you have seen so far, if we give up our life to follow Christ, who is in charge from that point on?

7 Beloved, let us love one another, for love is from God; and everyone who loves is born of God and knows God.

8 The one who does not love does not know God, for God is love.

9 By this the love of God was manifested in us, that God has sent His only begotten Son into the world so that we might live through Him.

10 In this is love, not that we loved God, but that He loved us

OBSERVE

What is the result of following Christ, of surrendering our life to Him? What is one of the defining characteristics of this new life? Let's look at the answer together.

Leader: Read 1 John 4:7–14.
   • *Have the group draw a heart over each occurrence of the word **love.***

Leader: Read through the passage again.
   • *This time have the group mark every reference to **God**, including synonyms and pronouns, with a triangle.*

DISCUSS

• According to verses 7 and 10, from where does love originate?

• Discuss what you learned about love from these verses.

and sent His Son to be the propitiation for our sins.

11 Beloved, if God so loved us, we also ought to love one another.

• Is this kind of love active or passive? Explain your answer.

12 No one has seen God at any time; if we love one another, God abides in us, and His love is perfected in us.

• Understanding what God did for us, how should we respond to others? Why?

13 By this we know that we abide in Him and He in us, because He has given us of His Spirit.

• What then is the mark of a believer?

14 We have seen and testify that the Father has sent the Son to be the Savior of the world.

• Since people can't see God, why is it so important that believers show love to them?

REVELATION 3:20

Behold, I stand at the door and knock; if anyone hears My voice and opens the door, I will come in to him and will dine with him, and he with Me.

OBSERVE

Leader: Read Revelation 3:20. Have the group...

> • *mark each pronoun referring to Jesus with a cross.*
>
> • *circle anyone and the pronouns referring to this person.*

DISCUSS

• What did you learn from marking *Jesus*?

• What does He want from you?

• Is Jesus knocking at the door of your heart?

• Do you believe in Him? Do you want to
  ask Him to come into your heart by faith
  and live there? Do you want to do it now?

WRAP IT UP

You have seen that the greatest command is to love God and the second is to love people. But you will never fulfill either one of these commandments unless you are a Christian, someone who has surrendered his or her life to God. When you make the choice to give control over to Him, God changes your heart and empowers you to be a lover of God and a lover of people.

If you want to be a Christian, there are two more things we want to say to you before you make that decision.

First, Christianity is a religion of surrender. To be a Christian is to surrender your life to God. Your whole life, and every aspect of it, is to be under the authority of God. In other words, you give up the right to be in charge of your own life.

Second, there is no guarantee in Scripture that your life will be smooth, simple, and pain-free once you become a Christian. In fact the opposite is true. Christians suffer and face trials like everyone else in this world. We are not exempt. However, as Christians we do have an edge: God Himself walks with us through the trials and difficulties of this life. He has even promised that He will never leave us.

If you want to become a Christian, then talk to God. Ask Him to forgive you for the things you have done wrong. Pray and ask Him to save you from the penalty you realize that you deserve. Surrender your life to Him, and ask Him to fill your very being with His presence. Do it today, do it now. He stands at the door and knocks. Let Him come in.

Leader: *You might lead anyone who wants to be a Christian in this prayer:*

Father, I realize I have done things that were wrong, things that caused me to miss Your standard of righteousness. Would You forgive me? Would You apply the payment Jesus made on the cross to the penalty that I owe? I completely surrender my life to You. You will be the one in charge in my life from now on. Fill me with Your presence. Thank You for saving me.

If you just prayed that prayer, it is very important that you tell someone, such as your small-group leader. You need to say out loud to someone that you just made this decision. They will help you in this new walk.

Welcome to the family. Praise the Lord!

As God has loved us, so we as Christians should be loving the people He has placed in our lives. Loving God and loving people should define your entire life. On these two commands the church stands.

Go out today and let your light—your love—shine before men that they see your good works and glorify your Father who is in heaven (Matthew 5:16).

40 MINUTE BIBLE STUDIES

No-Homework

That Help You

A 6-WEEK, NO-HOMEWORK BIBLE STUDY
MORE THAN 700,000 SOLD IN THE SERIES

Being a Disciple:
Counting the Real Cost

Kay Arthur, Tom & Jane Hart

A 6-WEEK, NO-HOMEWORK BIBLE STUDY
MORE THAN 700,000 SOLD IN THE SERIES

Building a Marriage **That Really Works**

Kay Arthur, David & BJ Lawson

A 6-WEEK, NO-HOMEWORK BIBLE STUDY
MORE THAN 700,000 SOLD IN THE SERIES

How to Make Choices **You Won't Regret**

Kay Arthur, David & BJ Lawson

A 6-WEEK, NO-HOMEWORK BIBLE STUDY
MORE THAN 700,000 SOLD IN THE SERIES

A Man's Strategy
For Conquering Temptation

Bob Vereen

A 6-WEEK, NO-HOMEWORK BIBLE STUDY
MORE THAN 700,000 SOLD IN THE SERIES

Living **Victoriously in Difficult Times**

Kay Arthur, Bob & Diane Vereen

A 6-WEEK, NO-HOMEWORK BIBLE STUDY
MORE THAN 700,000 SOLD IN THE SERIES

Discovering
What the Future Holds

11 59

Kay Arthur & Georg Huber

A 6-WEEK, NO-HOMEWORK BIBLE STUDY
MORE THAN 700,000 SOLD IN THE SERIES

Living Like You Belong to God

Kay Arthur, David & BJ Lawson

A 6-WEEK, NO-HOMEWORK BIBLE STUDY
MORE THAN 700,000 SOLD IN THE SERIES

Key Principles of Biblical Fasting

Kay Arthur & Pete De Lacy

A 6-WEEK, NO-HOMEWORK BIBLE STUDY
MORE THAN 700,000 SOLD IN THE SERIES

Forgiveness:
Breaking the Power of the Past

Kay Arthur, David & BJ Lawson

Bible Studies
Discover Truth For Yourself

Another powerful study series
from beloved Bible teacher

KAY ARTHUR

The Lord series provides insightful, warm-hearted Bible studies designed to meet you where you are—and help you discover God's answers to your deepest needs.

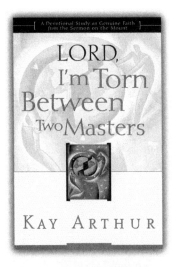

[A Devotional Study on Genuine Faith from the Sermon on the Mount]

LORD, I'm Torn Between Two Masters

KAY ARTHUR

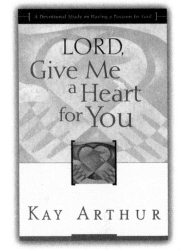

[A Devotional Study on Having a Passion for God]

LORD, Give Me a Heart for You

KAY ARTHUR

[A Devotional Study on God's Care and Deliverance]

LORD, Heal My Hurts

KAY ARTHUR

ALSO AVAILABLE:
One-year devotionals to draw you closer to the heart of God.

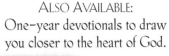

Lord, I Give You This Day

KAY ARTHUR

Search My Heart, O God

KAY ARTHUR

ABOUT KAY ARTHUR AND PRECEPT MINISTRIES INTERNATIONAL

KAY ARTHUR is known around the world as an international Bible teacher, author, conference speaker, and host of the national radio and television programs *Precepts for Life*, which reaches a worldwide viewing audience of over 94 million. A four-time Gold Medallion Award–winning author, Kay has authored more than 100 books and Bible studies.

Kay and her husband, Jack, founded Precept Ministries International in 1970 in Chattanooga, Tennessee, with a vision to establish people in God's Word. Today, the ministry has a worldwide outreach. In addition to inductive study training workshops and thousands of small-group studies across America, PMI reaches nearly 150 countries with inductive Bible studies translated into nearly 70 languages, teaching people to discover Truth for themselves.

Contact Precept Ministries International for more information about inductive Bible studies in your area.

Precept Ministries International
P.O. Box 182218
Chattanooga, TN 37422-7218
800-763-8280
www.precept.org

ABOUT DAVID AND BJ LAWSON

DAVID AND BJ LAWSON have been involved with Precept Ministries International since 1980. After nine years in the pastorate, they joined PMI full-time as directors of the student ministries and staff teachers and trainers. A featured speaker at PMI conferences and in Precept Upon Precept videos, David writes for the Precept Upon Precept series, the New Inductive Study Series, and the 40-Minute Bible Studies series. BJ has written numerous 40-Minute Bible Studies and serves as the chief editor and developer of the series. In addition she is a featured speaker at PMI women's conferences.